This journal belongs to ...

To my strong, kind, spectacular daughters. May you always know your north and lead the way.

© Copyright 2022

Title: The pre-teen friendship journal
Author: Fiona Ghiglione, Ph.D.
Cover Artwork: Fanny Ozda
Photography: Anastasia Shuraeva
ISBN: 978-0-6456099-0-5
Website: www.motheringgirls.com
Email: fiona@motheringgirls.com

Copyright remains the property of the author and apart from fair dealings for the purpose of study, research, criticism, or review, as permitted under the Copyright Act, no part of this publication may be reproduced, stored in a retrieval system, or transmitted in any form or by any means, electronic, mechanical, photocopying, recording or otherwise, without written permission. All enquiries should be made to fiona@motheringgirls.com

Disclaimer

The material in this publication is of the nature of general comment only and does not represent professional advice. it is not intended to provide specific guidance for particular circumstances and it should not be relied on as the basis of any decision to take action or not take action on any matter which it covers. Readers should obtain professional advice where appropriate, before making any such decision. To the maximum extent permitted by law, the author and publisher disclaim all responsibility and liability to any person, arising directly or indirectly from any person taking or not taking action based on the information in this publication.

WELCOME
WONDERFUL GIRL!

Do you ever feel a bit stuck in your friendships? Do you ever wish you could just wave a magic wand and you'd have a group of awesome friends by your side? If you said yes, this book is for you!

I believe that you have some very special things to offer the world and want to help you find those friends who value you for you!

In this journal there are many tips and exercises to tackle lots of common challenges in friendships e.g. being ourselves, meeting new friends, overcoming friendship hiccups, setting boundaries and much more.

There are two different ways you can use this journal - you can work through it from cover to cover OR whenever you face a moment with your friends that feels hard, you can jump to the section that you feel like you want to work through.

Try the exercises and give them some time to work. Sometimes they'll help the first time you try them and sometimes they might need a bit of patience and practice to work their magic.

Whatever happens - keep believing that beautiful friends are possible! Because you deserve it and have got this!

Fiona xx

CONTENTS

Welcome 8

Be You! 9

Find Your People 26

Meeting Friends 39

Choosing Friends to Invest in 52

Building Friendships 58

Navigating Friendship Hiccups 87

The Friendship Pivot 124

Journal 130

Welcome to the Friendship journey!

We are all on a journey... to find our TRUE FRIENDS! Those awesome people who we love; who laugh with us; who accept us as we are and are there when we need them.

This journey may sometimes feel hard and long - and will require us to be brave, patient & strong - but will be worth all the effort in the friends we find!

Are you ready to start?

What do these three pictures have in common?

They are all originals! Meaning, that there is only one of them in the world. They are different and unique. And in fact, people take special care of them and LOVE them for their originality.

What is something you like that is original? e.g. A famous place you have visited, a song or book you love?

Be You!

You too are an original, a one-and-only. And you have your own special things to offer the world.

The world would be boring if we were all the same! Imagine a world made up of 7 billion identical people! Yikes!

So give yourself permission to be exactly you! And let everyone else get busy being themselves!

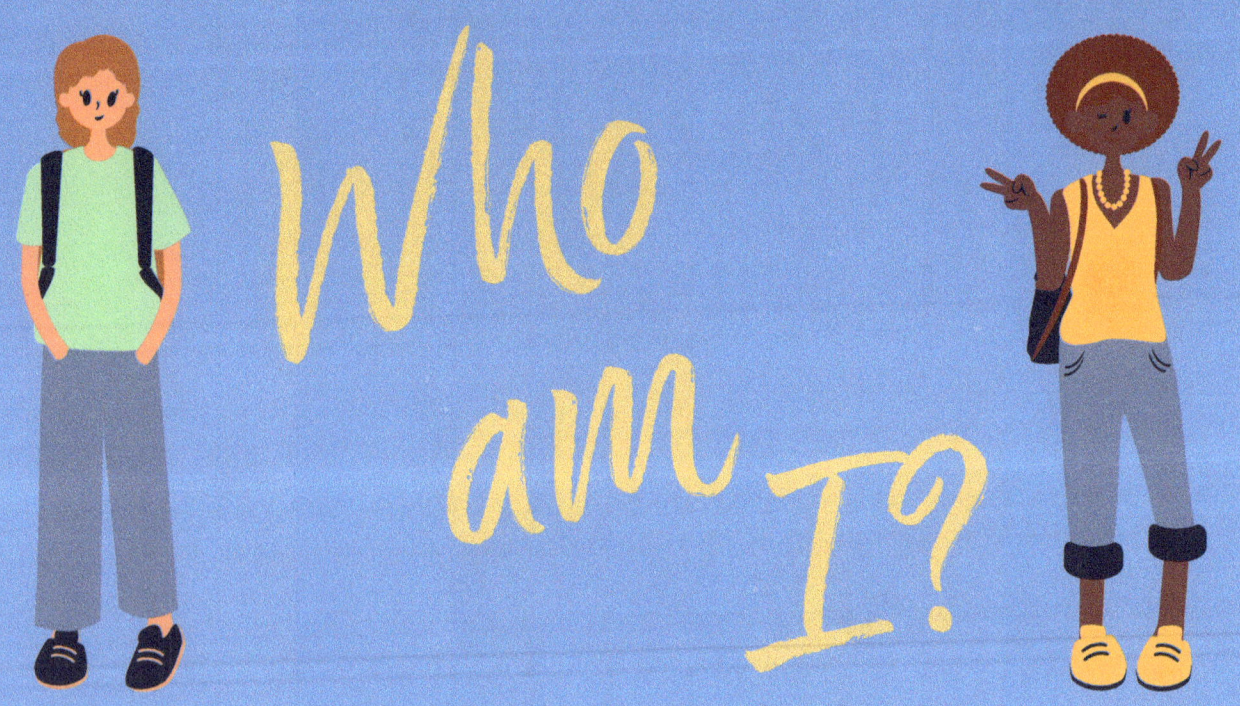

Who am I?

To have awesome friendships, we need to start by showing up as ourselves, in all our originality.

If we start a friendship PRETENDING to be someone we aren't then it'll be hard to make true friends (and it's exhausting!)

So, to start this journey, let's get to know the amazing you!

22 Things About Me

#1. I love:

#2. I don't like:

#3. My best vacation ever was:

#4. I believe in...

#5. I want to go to...

#6. My favourite movie & TV SHOW

22 Things About Me

#7. My favourite music/singer is

#8. My favourite book is

#9. My favourite thing to do with my family

#10. My favourite year in school so far

#11. A food that I crave is

#12. I love to talk about

22 Things About Me

#13. Something I worry most about is

#14. Something I dream about is

#15. Something I find relaxing is

#16. If I could meet a famous person it would be

#17. One of my biggest challenges right now is

#18. Something I love doing in my spare time is

22 Things About Me

#19. A cool experience I have had is

#20. My favourite subject at school is

#21. A pet hate (something that annoys me) is

#22. Something interesting about me is

Highlight or tick the words that describe you the most!

- Adaptable
- Adept
- Adventurous
- Affectionate
- Ambitious
- Artistic
- Assertive
- Authentic
- Approachable
- Balanced
- Bright
- Broad-minded
- Candid
- Cheerful
- Chill
- Clever
- Communicative
- Compassionate
- Competitive
- Charismatic
- Considerate
- Constructive
- Courageous
- Creative
- Curious
- Dependable
- Determined
- Direct
- Dynamic
- Easygoing
- Eclectic
- Emotional
- Energetic
- Enthusiastic
- Extroverted
- Exuberant
- Fearless
- Flexible
- Forgiving
- Friendly
- Fun
- Funny
- Generous
- Genuine
- Joyful
- Happy
- Helpful
- Honest
- Imaginative
- Independent
- Risk-taker
- Intuitive
- Inventive
- Inspiring
- Knowledgeable
- Kind
- Logical
- Loyal
- Loving
- Mature
- Modest
- Motivated
- Open-minded
- Optimistic
- Original
- Outgoing
- Passionate
- Patient
- Perceptive
- Persistent
- Pleasant
- Practical
- Reliable
- Respectful
- Responsible
- Self-reliant
- Sensible
- Sincere
- Sociable
- Shy
- Straightforward
- Strong
- Successful
- Sympathetic
- Thoughtful
- Tolerant
- Tough
- Trustworthy
- Understanding
- Upbeat
- Versatile
- Vibrant
- Warmhearted
- Wise

GET CREATIVE AND STICK THINGS ON THIS PAGE THAT SHOW WHO YOU ARE! E.G. PHOTOS, STICKERS, TICKETS TO PLACES YOU'VE BEEN, NOTES TO YOURSELF!

MAKE IT YOUR OWN!

What is one of the best experiences you have had?
(E.g. a holiday, something you did, a moment you remember)

5 things I am grateful for in my life right now are:

Describe one of your proudest moments. Who were you at that moment? What did you do?

What are your Top 10 Strengths?

Write words that describe the best parts of you. What qualities do you love and wouldn't want to change? E.g. I make people laugh, I am creative, I am kind.

Write about a person you admire. What qualities do you have in common with this person?

What is something you could do for hours? What makes you feel alive & relaxed?

FIND YOUR PEOPLE!

I love being with people who...

My go-to person/people are:

Who are your 'people'?

You can call them many different names - your tribe, crew or team. Whatever you call them, they are the people who you feel most at home with. Who you value, trust and who deeply care about you.

You already have so many people in your own personal crew or tribe! (Yes, you do!)

Parents, siblings, friends, aunts, cousins, grandparents, teachers, mentors, counsellors!

Who are your people?
Write their names in the circles!

Learn from Your Tribe!

Ask someone in your TRIBE (E.g. mum, grandma, aunt or mentor) these three questions! Write their answers below.

1. What were your friendships like in middle or primary school?

_____
_____
_____
_____
_____
_____

2. What do you love most about your friends?

3. What do you think are the hardest things in friendships?

Thanking Your Tribe

Write a letter or organize a thank you gift for those people who support you.

Pick up the phone and call to see how they are doing.

Sometimes just a small "thanks" or gesture can make their day!

Brainstorm things you could do to show them your appreciation!

What was it like to deliver the letter/gift or do something nice? How did it feel?

What did they say?

Expanding your Tribe

As you grow up, you will likely want to add more people to your tribe.

The rest of this journal is about how to find those special people (and know who they are or aren't).

DID YOU KNOW?

Sometimes it is easy to believe that getting LOTS of followers on social media or being the most popular girl in the school will bring us happiness - but will it? What does science tell us?

Many studies have shown that girls who had a small group of good friends at school grew up to be more resilient and happier than those who were popular.

They also found that if you have just one good friend by your side it can help you face life's challenges with more confidence!

In one study, researchers got people to stand at the bottom of a hill and asked if they thought they could climb it. Those people who had their friends by their side were more likely to feel they could!

So, building a few strong friendships can help us be healthier, feel more confident and have more fun.

WRITE A LETTER TO YOURSELF ABOUT THE KIND OF FRIENDSHIPS YOU WISH FOR YOURSELF!

Dear Me,

xx

THE STAGES OF FRIENDSHIPS

Meeting Friends

Choosing Friends to Invest In

Building Friendships

Navigating Friendship Hiccups

The Friendship Pivot

MEETING FRIENDS

It's really normal to sometimes worry about making good friends. Write down any worries you might have had about this.

Positive Friendship Affirmations

we can tell ourselves!

- I WILL FIND MY TRIBE
- I AM A GOOD FRIEND
- I AM INTERESTING
- I MATTER

Ideas for things that you can do to meet new friends!

Get classes for a new hobby

Join a sports team

Form a book club

Invite someone outside & get active

Join a like-minded community

Invite someone to sit with you at lunch

What are some ideas you could try to meet new friends?

_____
_____
_____
_____
_____
_____

Write down your positive affirmations!

_____
_____
_____
_____
_____
_____

Embrace the Awkward!

Sometimes meeting new people can be awkward!

We may not know what to say or might feel scared to show our real selves.

The thing is, there is a good chance the other person is feeling awkward too! We've all been there. You're not alone!

Here are some ideas on how to start awesome conversations. Take a look and see if you can find conversation starters that feel natural to you!

>>>

EASY CONVERSATION STARTERS

I love R&B, what's your favorite music?

Do you have any interesting hobbies?

Have you ever been to (the skate park)?

What was your best (holiday, trip)?

What did you do (on the weekend, vacation?)

What do you think about …(the game)?

Write down some questions you feel comfortable asking new people - to start a conversation!

TIPS FOR BEING A TOP COMMUNICATOR!

Put down your phone.

Take off your headphones

Be approachable (smile, uncross your arms, and make eye contact) and take an interest in others!

Introduce yourself to new people in the group. e.g. "Hi I'm Ella."

Be curious.. Ask open-ended questions. E.g. "How was your weekend?"

Don't forget to share a bit about yourself too. E.g. "I love that new song. Have you heard it?"

#KINDNESSMATTERS

Every day we make hundreds of choices.

How we act
What we say
How we say it

And every single choice we make - will have an impact on other people and ourselves.

Even if it is hard. Even if it is not the choice others would make ...

Be a leader. Be brave. Do the kind thing. Make a difference.

Have you ever been left out of something? What did it feel like?

_____
_____
_____
_____
_____
_____
_____

♥

Do something kind today at school. Describe what it felt like.

_____
_____
_____
_____
_____

WHAT DIFFERENT GROUPS ARE YOU IN?

Joining different groups is a great way to meet new friends, share different interests and have fun! E.g. dance, sports, after-school activities, church, and camps.

CHOOSING FRIENDS TO INVEST IN

Building friendships is a bit like building a house.

You can't expect to build it in a day.

First you need to set the foundations - the things that keep it strong - and then you build from there.

What qualities do you think 'good friends' have? e.g they are supportive, funny, kind? Write them here.

A GOOD FRIEND IS

♥ _____

♥ _____

♥ _____

♥ _____

♥ _____

♥ _____

♥ _____

TRUSTING KIND
LOYAL NO DRAMA
fun Patient
accepting
caring ♡
PRESENT
NON judgemental
Thoughtful
A GOOD LISTENER!
RELIABLE

Not everyone will like us; just like we won't like & click with everyone we meet.

And that is okay!

Let's save our energy for people who care about us and show good friendship qualities!

Take a moment to think about this: what kind of friend do you want to be remembered as? Imagine someone in the future talking about the kind of friend you were at school - how would you want them to describe you? e.g. generous, kind, funny.

BUILDING FRIENDSHIPS

Let's Start!

So you've met someone who seems nice and you think "they could be a good friend" or "I'd like to hang out with them more".

But you might be asking "how can I build this friendship?"

Good question!
Let's explore this!

Friendships are like all living things - they need to be nurtured and cared for and take time to grow!

Make it your mission to give your friendships a bit of love and care each week!

5 tips for nurturing our friendships!

#1 Speak Up & Share!

Sometimes, (especially in new friendships) we can feel worried or shy and decide to not share stuff about ourselves. Instead, we say things that we think <u>THEY</u> want to hear.

But if we want to make genuine and authentic friends we need to be okay with sharing things about ourselves, like:

Our interests
Our ideas
Our opinions
Our experiences
Stuff we care about.

Try this: next time you chatting with a friend and a topic you know or are interested in comes up, share your thoughts with them. Give it a try!

What I shared:

_____
_____
_____
_____
_____
_____

How it felt when I shared:

_____
_____
_____
_____

#2 Be Curious!

One of the best qualities in a good friend is being a good listener and caring about the other person.

Ask questions & listen to their answers. This shows you care!

What are some questions you could ask your friend?

_____
_____
_____
_____
_____
_____
_____

WHAT DO YOU KNOW ABOUT YOUR FRIEND?

What we see

- Who they spend time with.
- Their clothes & style
- Their walk.
- Their talk.
- Their gestures.
- How they act.

What we don't see

- Their beliefs
- What they are thinking
- How they are feeling
- Their real strengths (what they can do well)
- Life experiences (stuff that has happened in their life)
- All their likes/dislikes
- The things they find hard

THIS WEEK'S

Challenge

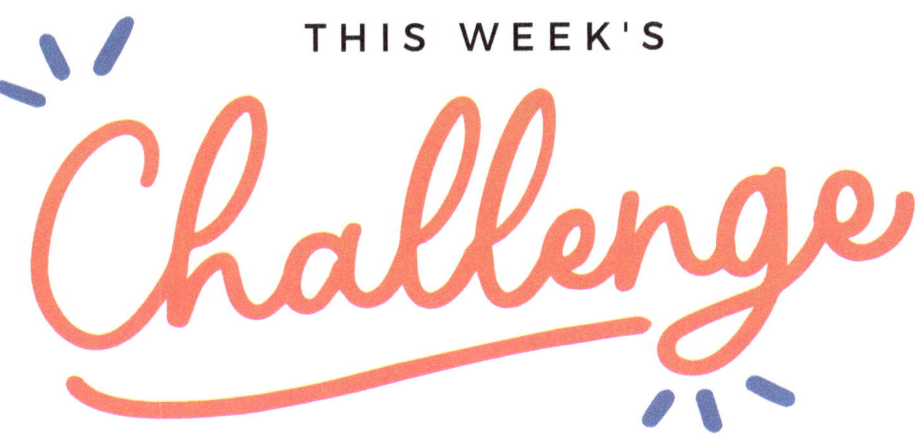

Write down some new things you learned about your friends this week!

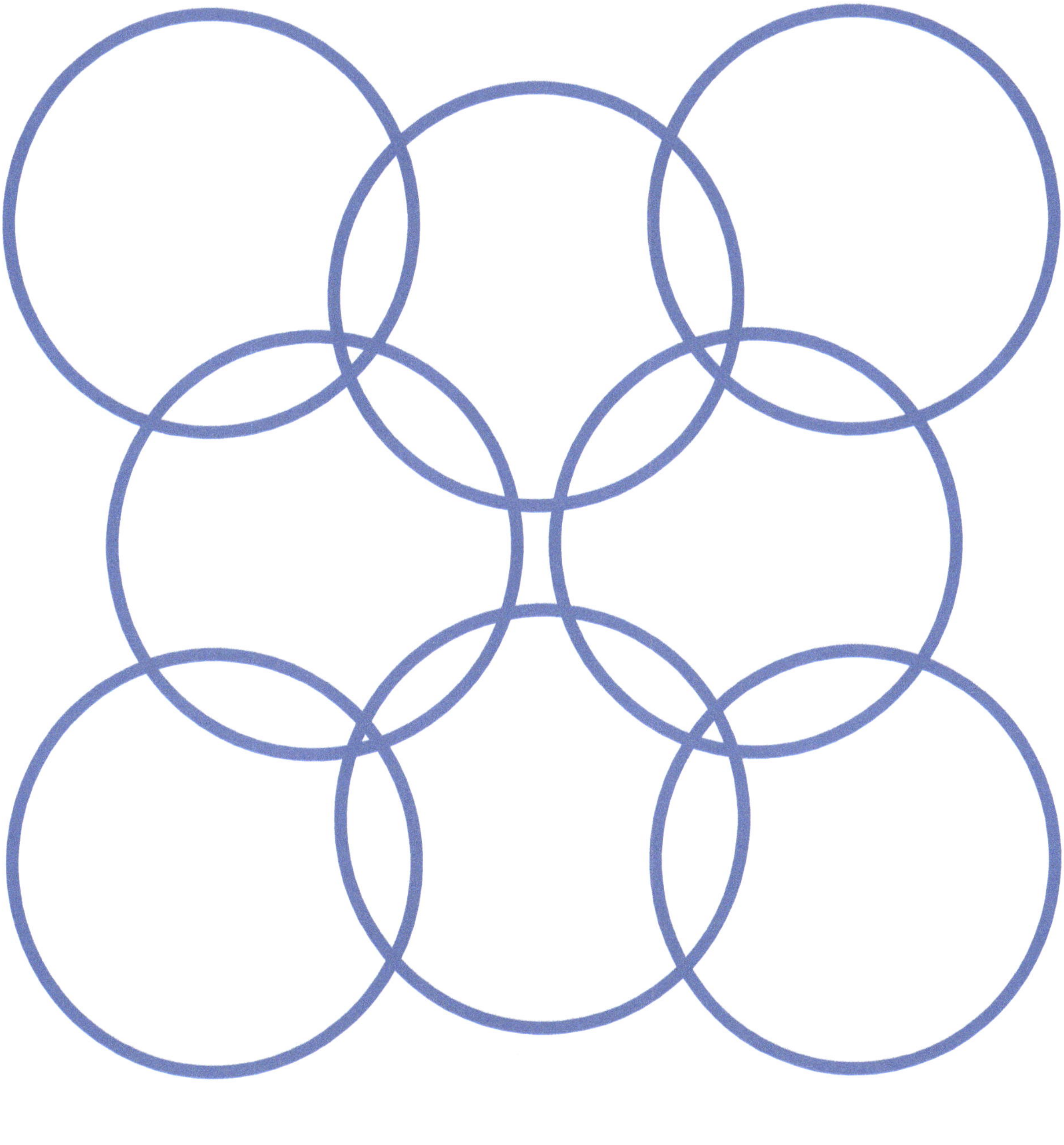

#3 Have Adventures

How do friendships grow? By spending time together and having new experiences!

Sure, looking at funny cat videos will make you laugh but it won't help you learn much about each other.

Actually, the more we stare at our screens, (even if it is together) the less time we are spending having other cool experiences that deepen our friendship.

What do you both like to do? What are some cool/exciting/fun things you could do together? E.g. go to the skatepark, swim at the beach, watch a movie, Go-carting.

What are some things you could do at home (when you can't go out)? E.g. cook, listen to music, shoot hoops outside, make ice cream.

Every day you can choose to spend hours scrolling and watching other people's lives

OR

make your own ADVENTURE

Add photo here

Add photo here

Fun with Friends

Add photo here

Add photo here

#4 Be Kind & Loyal

A big part of being kind as a friend is saying no to negative gossip! But what exactly is gossip? Gossip is a conversation about someone who isn't present. There are 3 types: positive, negative and neutral.

Positive: This type supports someone by talking about good things they've done or the kind of person they are.
E.g. "I hear she is an amazing athlete"

Neutral: This involves telling someone facts that are happening without judging.
E.g. "She had to leave early."

Negative: This type can hurt someone and damage their reputation and friendships.
E.g. "Bet she cheated on the test. How can she get such good marks?"

Imagine if you were the person being talked about. What would you feel like?

_____
_____
_____
_____
_____

What are some things you could do or say if you hear negative gossip?

_____
_____
_____
_____
_____

WAYS I CAN RESPOND WHEN I HEAR GOSSIP

1. CHANGE THE TOPIC!

2. SHRUG & GIVE IT NO ATTENTION.

3. FIND YOUR OWN RESPONSE

4. LET IT STOP WITH YOU. DON'T PASS IT ON!

EXAMPLES

- Why are you telling me this?
- Interesting, that's not what I know about her (insert your experience)
- Hey, that doesn't seem like our business.
- I'm not okay talking about this behind her back. Let's change the subject.

»—→ **IN A WORLD** ←—«

Where you can be anything

CHOOSE TO BE

Kind

KINDNESS challenge

Challenge yourself to four random acts of kindness this week. Write them below:

1. _____

2. _____

3. _____

4. _____

Reflection: What did giving feel like?
_____

#5 Be Appreciative

What is something you are grateful and appreciative for? Perhaps something your friend did or said? Big or small, remember to say thanks or show your friend that you appreciate them.

We are all human beings and make mistakes. No friendship will be perfect.

Each friend will offer us something different. We'll share different experiences, jokes, interests and conversation.

Let's look for the good in each friend and appreciate their uniqueness!

SMALL THINGS THAT NURTURE FRIENDSHIPS

Show your true self	Do something together	Check-in & ask about their day	Offer a hug or high five
Listen to them	Laugh together	Call them to chat (instead of texting)	Hang out
Share experiences together	Get to know about them	Give a thoughtful gift or message	Help them with something
Find your common interests	Say something supportive	Be happy to see them	Watch a movie you both like
Spend time together	Be consistent	Plan something together	Do the kindness challenge

So how do we know if a friendship is healthy or not?

Here are five things we can look for that give us clues as to whether our friendship is on the right track!

#1 You can trust each other.

How does your friend respond to the "smaller" things?

If you say, for example, "mum had to help me with maths" and she runs off to tell everyone; then you probably won't be able to trust her yet with the bigger things! (This applies to us too!)

Try confiding in your friend on the smaller stuff first! Remind them when something is confidential. We should be able to trust our friends with things, big and small.

#2 You enjoy spending time together.

After you spend time with her/him what do you notice?

Do you think, "Wow that was so much fun", "I really loved today" or "I can't wait until the next time we get together" (GOOD SIGN!)

Or do you think, "I didn't enjoy today" or "I feel so bad/sad when I'm with her/him" (NOT SUCH A GOOD SIGN!)

How you feel around each other most of the time is a good sign to know if it is a healthy friendship or not.

#3 You accept them and they accept you.

Do you feel ok being <u>ALL</u> of yourself with your friend (yes, EVEN your quirky qualities!)? Does your friend embrace all of you or do they feel embarrassed about things you do?

Are you accepting of your friend?

Good friends accept you as you are in this moment. They let you be yourself and don't try to change you into someone else.

#4 You want to share things with them.

Whenever something great happens, do you find yourself thinking "ooh, I've got to call...!"

Does your friend celebrate your successes and feel happy for you? If they do - that is a good sign!

We all take turns to have good things happen to us in our lives and healthy friendships include supporting each other & celebrating those wins.

#5 They think of you and are there for you.

When you are sad, upset, or down, does your friend listen?

Do you listen to them when they aren't feeling great?

We won't always be happy and smiling - sometimes we are sad, angry, and annoyed too.

Good friends know this and try to make time to be there for each other in these moments too!

NAVIGATING FRIENDSHIP HICCUPS

All friendships have some ups & downs.
You're not alone!

Our goal in friendships is to have more ups than downs and to give our friends (& ourselves) a chance to figure out those 'downs' together.

Let's look at some ways we can do that!

My Circle of Control

We can control some things but have less control over other things. Let's focus our attention on making amazing choices from within our circle of control!

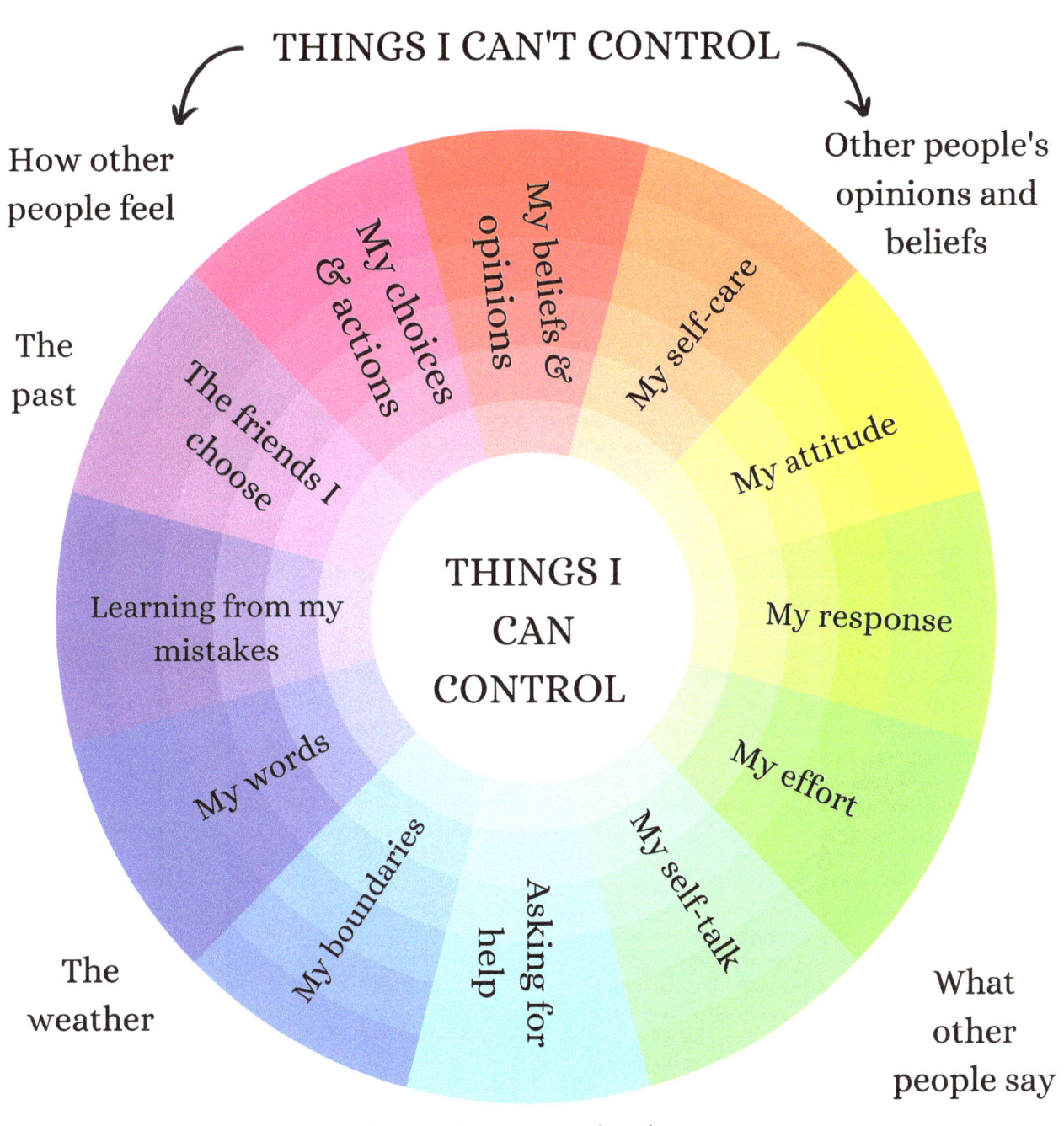

You are more powerful than you believe.

In every word you choose.
In every action you take.
In every thing you do.

You have the power to choose your reponse.

What are some things that your friends do (or don't do) that really upset you?

WHAT CAN I DO WHEN I FEEL WORRIED?

What if they are talking about me? What if she doesn't want to be my friend? What if….?

1. TAKE A DEEP BREATH & PRACTISE MINDFULNESS

2. ASK YOURSELF: WHAT EVIDENCE DO I HAVE?

3. TALK TO YOUR FRIEND!

4. GET BUSY AND COME BACK TO IT LATER. THEN SEE, DO YOU FEEL THE SAME?

EXAMPLES

- I noticed you didn't reply to my text; is everything okay?
- I'd love to spend some time together later and chat. Are you free?
- It seems as though you are angry/upset with me, is that right?

Sometimes our brains imagine what "might happen" if our friend gets upset with us. Have you ever had this happen? What kind of story does your mind think up when you have a fight with a friend?

1ST THOUGHT

"Oh no, I forgot to do my part in the group project!"

We have control over how we RESPOND to our thoughts! We can keep going with thoughts OR can use mindfulness to let them go & find a solution!

MORE THOUGHTS

"They will never forgive me!"

"I'm such a loser."

"I'm going to lose them as friends."

"I'm going to be alone."

Pause & Reflect

Instead of going down the spiral of second thoughts, which makes us feel worse - let's stop and think more about what's happening!

Think of a hard situation with a friend recently.
What happened? Describe it.

_____
_____
_____

How did it make you feel?
Rate that feeling (0 = mild; 10 = strong).

_____

What were you thinking? What thoughts passed through your mind?

_____
_____
_____

What evidence did you have that it was true?
Untrue? What other explanation could there be?

_____
_____

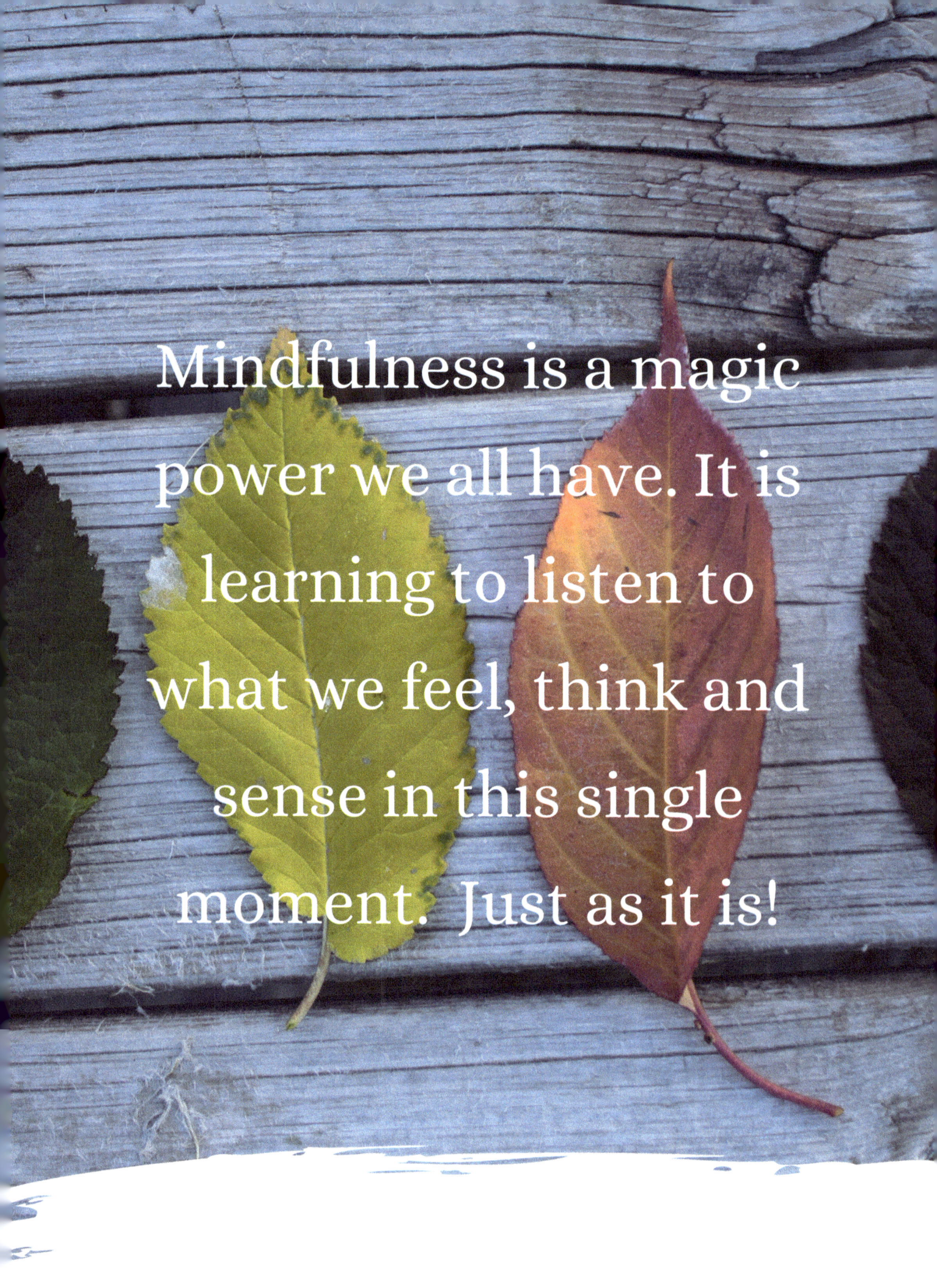

Mindfulness is a magic power we all have. It is learning to listen to what we feel, think and sense in this single moment. Just as it is!

In every tough moment with a friend, there is:

The Situation
What happened?
With who?
Where?

Our Thoughts
What thoughts do you have? What does this mean?

Our Feelings
What are you feeling? What do you notice in your body?

Our Response
What did you do?
How did you respond?

Mindfulness helps us understand ourselves better, feel calmer and make healthier decisions.

We can have so many feelings and emotions in our friendships. Sadness, anger, happiness, jealousy, confusion - the full rainbow!

Let's remember that our feelings won't be the same forever. They change all the time!

Mindfulness is being able to invite all our emotions in - one by one - and listen to what they are telling us! Let's use them to guide us in our friendships.

A MINDFUL BRAIN BREAK

Shifting our Attention

When we are worried our attention is stuck on our thoughts. It feels as though we can't do anything else except think and worry!

But you are in control of your brain! So, try this trick. Stop what you are doing and look around you. What do you see? Close your eyes. What do you smell? Listen. What do you hear? Take 10 minutes to shift your mind from your thoughts and drop into your senses. How do you feel now?

A MINDFUL BRAIN BREAK
Breath Tracing

When we breathe slower, we help our brains calm! So try this: trace your finger up one side of the star, while you take a deep breath in. Hold your breath at the point and breathe out as you slide down the other side. Keep going until you've gone around the whole star.

A MINDFUL BRAIN BREAK

Letting Go of Thoughts

Close your eyes and imagine your thought as a butterfly (or a bird). Let it sit on your finger (or your shoulder) for a bit and then let it go. Imagine it flying off into the air.

Do this as many times as you need. We will always have thoughts come into our minds. But we can choose how to respond! The more we do this, the easier it is to let go.

A MINDFUL BRAIN BREAK
Mindful Colouring

Take your time to add your own splash of colour.
Notice how you feel as you do this!

A MINDFUL BRAIN BREAK

Loving Kindness

Close your eyes and imagine yourself standing with a friend or someone you care about. Picture yourself standing together.

Take a moment now to consider this: despite our differences there are always things we have in common with others. We all have goals and dreams. We all just want to be happy and healthy and loved.

So stop for a moment and wish all of those things for yourself *and* your friend. Notice how it feels.

Other Ways To Relax
& CALM OUR MIND

Talk to someone (or get a hug)

Write in your journal

Practice gratitude

Breathe (In for 4. Hold for 6. Out for 7)

Get out in nature

Stretch with yoga

Listen to music

(The dreaded) FOMO!

It can be the worst feeling - seeing a picture of someone you thought was your friend at a party you weren't invited to. Or turning up to the lunch table and hearing everyone talking about something you didn't know about. It can make you feel worried, upset and really ... meh.

The thing is, these things can make us begin to worry and think, "What else am I going to miss out on?" It may even make you doubt yourself as a friend and person!

Fear of Missing Out (FOMO) can be a normal reaction - because we care about our friends and want to be loved and appreciated by them! But there are things we can do to deal with FOMO in a healthier way!

Try this:
- Remember sometimes you will be invited and sometimes you may not (and other people will be invited). Let's accept that this happens to us all.
- Take a break from social media for a bit. Take your phone out of your room (especially when you sleep!)
- Get out and do something you love. Invite another friend or someone from your tribe.

WHAT CAN I DO WHEN MY FRIEND TRIES TO PRESSURE ME TO DO (OR BE) SOMETHING I DON'T WANT?

Peer pressure can be positive or negative. When it is positive it can help us be our best. But sometimes, we feel pressured to do or say something just to be accepted by our friends e.g. cheating, taking dangerous risks, bullying others, or changing who we are. Here are ways we can respond to negative peer pressure:

1. LISTEN TO YOUR BODY. DOES THIS FEEL RIGHT?
2. MAKE AN EXCUSE. WALK AWAY.
3. FIND A MOMENT TO TELL THEM HOW YOU FEEL
4. TALK TO AN ADULT & TAKE TIME TO THINK.

EXAMPLES
- Sounds like you've already made up your mind but I need time to think about it.
- I feel upset when you tell me to do/not do that thing. It is part of who I am. I need you to stop saying that.
- You know, it's okay if we are different or believe different things.

WHAT CAN I DO WHEN MY FRIEND DOESN'T LIKE ME HAVING OTHER FRIENDS?

Fun fact: we don't own our friends and our friends don't own us! Sometimes you might have a friend who wants to spend time with you so much that they don't want us to spend any time with anyone else, which can feel stressful!
Here are some ways we can respond!

1. REASSURE THEM THAT YOU STILL VALUE THEIR FRIENDSHIP.

2. MAKE TIME TO SPEND WITH THEM

3. FIND YOUR OWN WORDS

4. STILL FIND TIME TO SPEND WITH OTHER FRIENDS

EXAMPLES

- It's okay for us to have different friends, but it doesn't mean I love our friendship less.
- Let's organise a time to hang out this week, but today I'm spending some time with my friend from dance.
- It's important to me that you are okay with us spending time with other friends too.

HELP! WHAT CAN I DO TO SAY NO TO MY FRIEND?

Many of us fear that we will lose our friends if we say no. But the reality is that in friendship there will always be times when we have to say no to stay safe and to keep our friendships healthy & respectful. So how do we do this?
Here are some ideas:

1 ASK THEM FOR SOME TIME TO SPEAK ALONE. IF YOU FEEL WORRIED, PLAN IT IN A PLACE WHERE YOU HAVE SUPPORT E.G. HOME

2 REMIND YOURSELF OF YOUR WHY. WHY IS THIS A NO FOR YOU?

3 FIND YOUR OWN RESPONSE (& PRACTICE SAYING IT OUT LOUD)

4 WRITE THEM A NOTE IF SPEAKING DIRECTLY IS TOO HARD.

EXAMPLES

- That doesn't feel right to me, so, no thanks.
- I need time to think about it. Ask me again next week.
- No, thank you.
- I'm not comfortable with that.
- Let me talk with my parents and I'll tell you later.

More ways to say 'no' and set boundaries!

- Since we went to your house last time, I'd love to go to mine this time.

- I feel too upset to talk about this anymore. Let's talk more about this on the weekend. Okay?

- That's a no from me today. I just don't feel comfortable about that.

- I'd love to hang out right now, but I have a lot of homework to catch up on. How about tomorrow?

- I love hanging out with you - you're one of my closest friends - but I also have to see some of my other friends too. I hope you understand.

- I want to help you with your note taking but it's not something I can do every week. Sorry.

- Going to the movies with you is so fun, I love it. But I don't enjoy time playing Minecraft as much. Let's find some other fun things we can do together.

Write down something that happened in your friendship. E.g. something someone said or did. How ok/not ok are you about it?
(Mark with an X)

OK   NOT OK

e.g (What happened) My friend stole & ate my lunch

Not that cool with it! Wish he'd ask.

Now your turn!

What happened: ....

What happened: ....

What happened: ....

What happened: ....

Let's revisit how we wanted to be remembered as friends! (Look at page 57!) Here are different actions we can choose to take. Circle the ones you think fits the kind of friend you want to be!

Ignoring others

Offering help

Complimenting someone

Asking how someone is

Smiling at someone who needs it

Including others

Saying thanks

Whispering

Laughing at someone

Standing up to bullies

Excluding people

Embarrassing people

Sharing photos without permission

Listening calmly

WHAT CAN I DO IF I SEE MY FRIEND BEING BULLIED?

When we see someone being mean over and over again (saying, doing or excluding) to try and hurt the other person, chances are it is bullying. Bullying can happen online or in real life. Either way, bullying is never okay! Let's be upstanders and help our friends in need. Here are some ways we can do this!

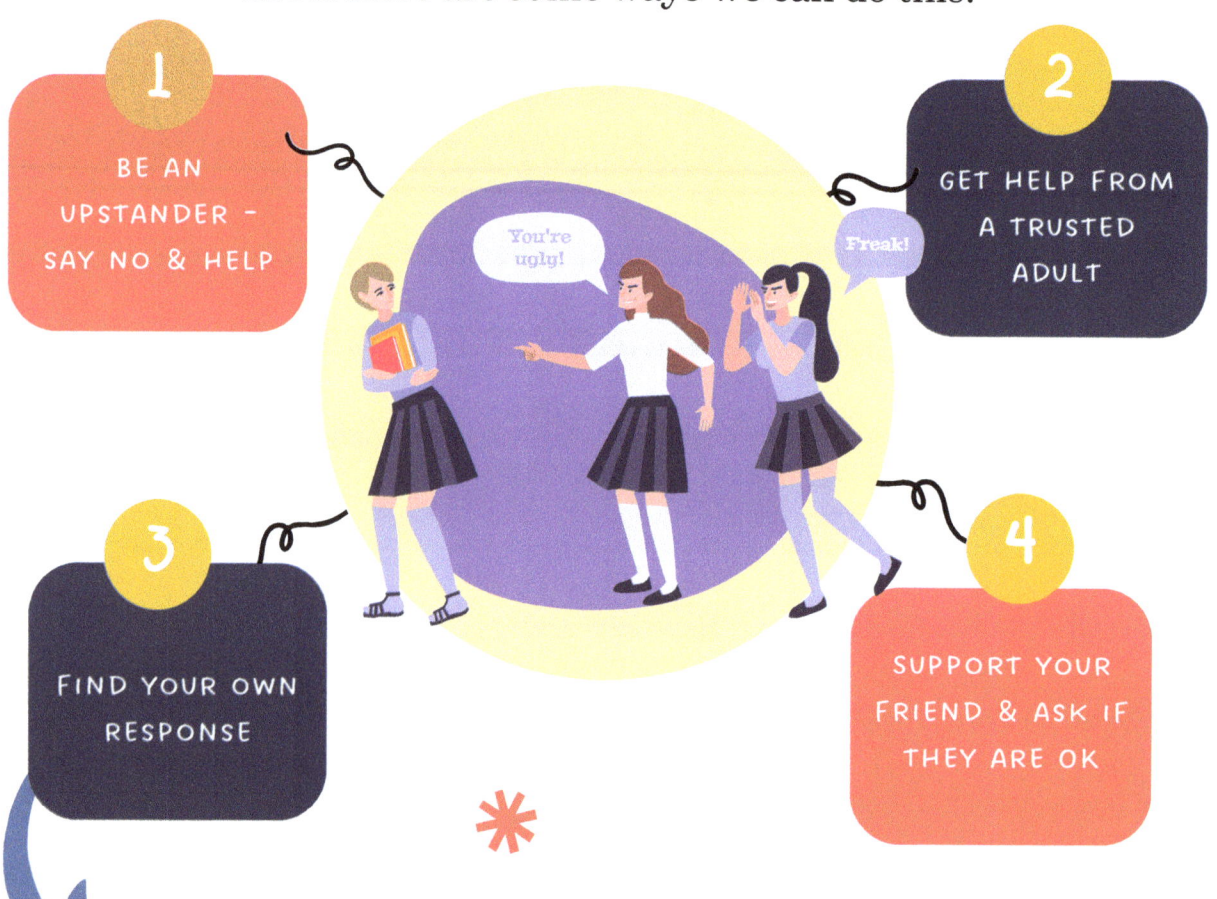

1. BE AN UPSTANDER - SAY NO & HELP
2. GET HELP FROM A TRUSTED ADULT
3. FIND YOUR OWN RESPONSE
4. SUPPORT YOUR FRIEND & ASK IF THEY ARE OK

Examples

- (To your friend) Want to come and hang out with me? or Come on, let's go.
- (To the bully) Hey - stop! That's not cool.. knock it off!
- (To a trusted adult) My friend needs help.

Be an up-stander.
Be that girl!

The one who asks if you are okay.

The one who says no to bullying.

The one who gets help.

WHAT CAN I DO IF I AM BEING BULLIED BY MY FRIEND?

1. BE CLEAR AND TELL HER IT ISN'T OK
2. ASK A TRUSTED ADULT FOR HELP*
3. FIND YOUR OWN RESPONSE
4. WALK AWAY
5. TAKE A SCREEN SHOT OF THE CONVERSATION/COMMENTS. THEN LEAVE THE GROUP CHAT OR MUTE YOUR FRIEND*

EXAMPLES

- I don't like it, please stop now.
- This is not how friends treat each other. I need you to stop doing this.
- I feel hurt right now. Please stop.
- (Use sarcasm) Yeah tell me when you get to the funny part.
- Remind yourself - bullying is never okay!

Next time you have a friendship conflict:

What are you feeling?
Write them down!

Your feelings are valid. They are trying to tell you something important! Listen to them.

IF YOU ARE UNSURE, IT IS PROBABLY A NO.

Listening to Ourselves!

When we feel stressed, our bodies react in different ways. E.g. our heart and breathing might get faster. It's our body's way of sending us a message - to take care of ourselves or maybe set a limit. So let's listen to our bodies! Next time you are stressed - what do you notice in your body? Draw it below.

Saying what you want and need is important in friendship.

Every friendship is different & the boundaries we set are different.

For example, with one friend we may need a bit more time alone and with another friend, we may need more time to hang out. Take some time to think about each of your friendships!

Next time you have a fight with your friend. What do you want? What do they want? Listen to each other. Write it here.

I want/need:

_____
_____
_____
_____

They want/need:

_____
_____
_____
_____

Everyone deep down wants to be loved, happy, and accepted. (Yes, even the mean girl at school).

So let's step into someone else's shoes for a moment and think: what would it be like to be them right now? What are they going through?

A big part of working out disagreements is finding the right thing to say! That means finding words that say what *you* need (while *also* being respectful to the other person). When we do this we are practicing something called assertive speaking.

So what words can we use? Try:

"I feel (name your emotion e.g. angry) when you (name what they did e.g. ignore me). I need you to (name what you need, e.g. tell me if you are upset)."

"I think we are misunderstanding each other, let's take a break for a moment and start again"

Before you speak, text or post - ask yourself...

Is what I am going to say:

Kind?

Helpful?

Inspiring?

Necessary?

The Right time?

Words that feel comfortable to me to say what I want and need:

Find the Words and Practice, Practice!

Say it in front of the mirror - the more you practice the easier it will be. Or ask your parents, sibling or another friend to role-play it so you get a chance to hear it out loud.

THE FRIENDSHIP PIVOT

Occasionally in our friendships - despite so much effort to be a good friend and to fix things - our friends still may choose *not* to treat us kindly.

Or may decide they don't want to be friends anymore.

Even though these moments can feel devastating, sometimes the best decision is to <u>pivot</u> and change course on our friendship journey.

What does it look like to pivot and do something differently? Here are 3 things you can do today!

Ask someone in your tribe to help you make a plan! Ask them for ideas on how to tell your friend or how to start afresh.

Take a break from spending time with that 'friend' and focus your time and attention on building other friendships.

Go and do things that makes you happy and fulfilled. Write a list of what those things are and tick them off!

Talk to Your Trusted Adult/s

There will be times when we need extra help on this journey and that's where our tribe comes in. Take some time to chat with your trusted adults!

My trusted adults suggested:

If you still need the support of another listening ear, try:

Kids Help Line Australia

1800 55 1800

Childhelp USA

1-800 422 4453

Kidsline NZ

0800 543 754

Tinkle Friend Helpline Singapore

1800 2744 788

Childline UK

0800 1111

or find a helpline in your country.

You are stronger than you believe.
Wiser than you think.
And 100% deserve beautiful friends.

There are so many people out there waiting to meet you. To be your friend.
Don't give up!

THE JOURNAL

JOURNAL REFLECTIONS

Date:

JOURNAL REFLECTIONS

Date:

Friendship Plan

Date:
S / M / T / W / T / F / S

PLANS WITH FRIENDS

Day:
_____

Friend's Name:
_____

What we will do:
_____
_____
_____

How it went:
_____
_____
_____

TODAY I WILL:

THINGS I'M GRATEFUL FOR IN MY FRIENDSHIPS

1.
2.
3.
4.
5.

MY AFFIRMATIONS

Friendship Plan

Date:
S / M / T / W / T / F / S

PLANS WITH FRIENDS

Day:
_____

Friend's Name:
_____

What we will do:
_____
_____
_____

How it went:
_____
_____
_____

TODAY I WILL:

_____
_____
_____
_____
_____
_____
_____
_____
_____
_____

THINGS I'M GRATEFUL FOR IN MY FRIENDSHIPS

1.
2.
3.
4.
5.

MY AFFIRMATIONS

www.ingramcontent.com/pod-product-compliance
Lightning Source LLC
Chambersburg PA
CBHW061137010526
44107CB00069B/2974